Building Your Successful Handyman Business:

A guide to starting and operating a profitable business

By Chuck Solomon
2010 Edition

BONUS: 65 customizable business forms and templates included with the purchase of this guide.

Building Your Successful Handyman Business:

A guide to starting and operating a profitable business

By Chuck Solomon
2010 Edition

Edited by Susan Siegel

Purchasers of the guide also receive online access to 65 forms and templates, which can be customized for their particular business.

Topics covered in this guide include:

I. Marketing and Sales

II. Operations

III. Finance and Administration

For additional information, please visit:
www.buildhandymanbusiness.com

For information regarding permission to reproduce sections of this book please contact:
permissions@buildhandymanbusiness.com

ISBN: 978-1448633524

Bonus: Access to 65 customizable business forms and templates included with the purchase of this guide book. See page 61 for access instructions.

In addition to this guide, other services are available from the author and include: business coaching and consulting, workshop and seminar presentations. Learn more at www.buildhandymanbusiness.com.

Acknowledgements

I want to thank the many people who reviewed this guide and offered suggestions and feedback. It is a better product because of your input. In particular, I thank my family, who gave me the encouragement, support and time to complete this task.

Also, a special note of thanks to those who purchased my earlier publication, *How To Start A Successful Handyman Business* on CD ROM, and offered their constructive comments and feedback. I used that feedback to build upon and produce this current edition.

This guide reflects what has worked for me in building my own business. My hope is that readers can take what I present and build their own successful handyman or home improvement businesses.

Your comments and feedback on this edition are more then welcome.

Best regards!
Chuck Solomon
November, 2009

Disclaimer

This guide, free templates, and associated website and the information contained therein are presented for "informational purposes only". It is not to be construed as legal, accounting or other professional advice. There is no warranty or guarantee offered as to the accuracy or completeness of any information provided. Laws and regulations change over time, and there are differences depending on jurisdiction, so it is best to consult an attorney and/or Certified Public Accountant for legal or accounting advice related to your particular business. Further, there is no guarantee of profitability or success with readers' own businesses. Efforts were made to ensure that web links were up-to-date prior to the publication of this guide; however, any link or referenced information is the responsibility of its respective publisher or owner.

TABLE OF CONTENTS

I. Marketing and Sales

II.   Operations

III.   Finance and Administration

Building Your Successful Handyman Business

Introduction

Congratulations on making the decision to purchase this guide. My hope is that you can put into practice the lessons of this guide to start and/or grow your own handyman, home improvement, or contracting business. I will be using those terms interchangeably throughout the book so that the widest possible audience of readers will find the information relevant to their goals. My goal is to help contractors be better business people.

The three sections of this guide include:

- Marketing and Sales
- Operations
- Finance and Administration

This guide is not a 'get rich quick' scheme, but a framework for starting and running a successful service business. Success in business, like success in anything you do, will be determined by the amount of time and effort you put into it.

Readers may have questions before they delve into this guide, and I will answer some common questions here.

Why did I write this guide?
I wrote this guide to share what has and hasn't worked for me over the past seventeen years of running my own business, so that others may benefit from my experience to learn the business side of contracting. Many individuals, contractors included, have little or no training or experience in starting and operating a successful business. This is a recipe for failure. An individual may be working in the trades sector for someone else and decide to go out on his or her own. I applaud those people, but encourage them to get the help and support they need.

My goal in writing this guide is to help great contractors become great business people. The sad truth is that many contractors, while greatly skilled at their respective trades, are not the best business people. This is clearly evidenced by the large number of contracting businesses that go out of business each year. The good news is that business skills, like any skills, can be learned and developed. This guide is designed to help build better business skills.

What qualifies the author?
This guide builds on my earlier work, *How To Start A Successful Handyman Business,* which was published in 2005.

I started my handyman business differently from most contractors. I was a white-collar professional who became a blue-collar business owner. Earning a bachelor's degree in business and psychology and a master's degree in human services administration provided me with excellent education and training for my current profession. I have helped to start and operate several successful organizations, and established my own home-improvement contracting business in 1992.

Most contractors are great at trade skills and have to learn the business side. I, however, was great at the business side and had to learn the trade skills. Success in this business depends on excelling at both trade skills AND business skills.

Who is the target audience for this book?
This book is for anyone who wants to operate a successful handyman/home improvement/contracting business in the United States or Canada, whether starting a brand-new business or expanding an existing one. The focus is on starting a small business or developing systems that will

help a small business to be more productive AND more profitable.

The information contained in this book is geared toward the handyman business. However, it can also benefit current or prospective owners of other businesses such as painting, plumbing, contracting, landscaping, electrical contracting, HVAC, paving & grading, power-washing, gutter cleaning, foundation, window cleaning, pool and spa, remodeling, masonry, chimney sweeping, flooring, tiling, site preparation, carpentry, and windows & siding.

A handyman/home improvement business is primarily a customer service business. To be successful, the principals must always focus on delivering great customer service. Delivering a superior handyman service but providing inferior customer service typically means few or no repeat customers.

What is the author's goal for readers when they are done reading the guide?
The goal of the author is to help contractors become more successful business people. A successful business can be profitable, achieve a high level of customer satisfaction, and be rewarding for the owner and employees. Like most things in life, business success requires tenacity and a lot of hard work.

Why did you order the book this way (marketing, operations, financial)?
Generally, the typical business cycle starts with marketing to attract customer, then providing the service (operations), and then keeping track of everything (financial and administration). Each component of the guide is equally important, and they may be read out of order as stand-alone chapters. Business owners need to perform each of these

tasks (marketing, operation, financial) frequently and consistently, as much as every week or even every day to be successful.

Does this guide cover topics related to handyman franchisers?
This book is not intended for those who wish to purchase a handyman franchise or other home improvement business franchise. A handyman franchise offers buyers a complete business system with considerable cost, but it also may produce considerable benefits. Most franchisors will have a business prospectus, and it is prudent to thoroughly review all of the information.

Is access to a computer and computer software required to use this guide?
Although the information here will be useful to anyone wishing to start a handyman/home improvement business, the online resources and templates do require computer access. Also, having the commonly used computer software programs from Microsoft including MS Word and MS Excel would be helpful as well. The instructions throughout this guide are written for Windows computer users.

Your comments and constructive feedback about this guide are welcome and encouraged, so that I may continue to update and improve the information. Feel free to email me at: chuck@buildhandymanbusiness.com.

Also, be sure to check the website frequently for updates and additional resources to build your business: www.buildhandymanbusiness.com

I am also available for consulting services to help you start your home repair business or bring it to the next level. Please email me to learn more.

Best wishes and much success in your handyman business!

Chuck Solomon

Marketing and Sales

Do not let what you cannot do interfere with what you can do. - John Wooden

Marketing: Promoting and Selling

Each and every aspect of your home improvement business is important. However, if you don't market your business to produce sales, then you won't have a business for very long. This section will take you through the process of promoting and selling your services to customers.

A typical sales process for a home improvement business follows these steps:

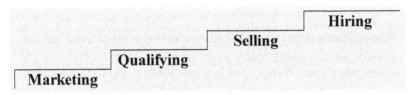

The pages that follow will discuss each of these steps in greater detail; marketing, qualifying, selling and getting hired.

Marketing Your Service Business

According to the Merriam-Webster Dictionary, marketing is defined as the process of promoting and selling a product or service. Marketing a service-based business is more difficult than selling a product. When a customer buys a product, it is tangible – something you can see, touch, or hold, and that can usually be returned if the customer is not satisfied. With a service business, however, your customers are buying something that is intangible and not returnable. One of the greatest challenges in marketing your service business is persuading people to buy something they can't see, smell, touch, or return. You are selling both yourself and your skills, and selling the value of the services that you provide.

Marketing is the single most important skill needed to be successful in the home improvement business. It involves promoting your company and its services to both immediate and potential customers, and selling your services to those that have found you through your advertising efforts. You will also market your home improvement business by providing quality work and a high level of customer service, which will encourage repeat customers and word-of-mouth referrals.

The primary objective of your marketing efforts is to have a steady stream of current and prospective customers contacting you. Your goal is to be able to sell your services to those customers.

The words 'marketing' and 'advertising' are often used interchangeably. Advertising is one aspect of the marketing strategy that helps you promote your business in the marketplace. Various advertising strategies, as well as examples of strategies to market a home improvement business, will be presented in detail later in this guide.

Market Research

Many books have been written on the topic of market research, and you are encouraged to do further reading on the topic. Essentially, market research is about understanding your competition, determining your target audience, and defining your geographic area of service. Understanding your local market, your customer profiles, and what your competitors are doing will help inform your business. In order to stay competitive, a successful home improvement business will undertake either formal or informal market research on an ongoing basis.

Qualifying Customers

Some people are natural salespeople, while others have to work at it. No matter which category you fall under, there is an abundance of material written to improve your skills in sales and selling. In addition to following this guide, a person new to selling should read other sales materials and attend sales training and seminars. The more you learn, the better a sales person you will become.

As previously noted, a typical sales process for a home improvement business requires the following steps.

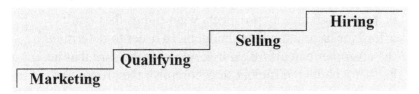

Through your marketing efforts, you are attracting people with a home repair or home improvement need. Then through qualifying, you are ensuring that your prospective customer has the money and the motivation to hire you to get his or her project done.

Qualifying means to ensure that someone will make a good customer. Not everyone who contacts you will make a good customer, so it is best to assess the prospective customer's 'qualities' before deeming them appropriate to do business with your company. Qualifying is very important, as you only have so much time and energy for selling. You want to be sure that you are selling to the most appropriate individuals. The Operations section of this guide has a discussion on "What jobs to avoid" that will further help you to qualify prospective customers.

Much of the work of selling is learning about your customers, understanding their needs, and determining whether or not they are qualified to buy what you are selling. This last step is crucial. If they are not qualified, then it doesn't matter if you can sell your services, as they do not have the ability to buy them. Each business will need to define for itself what a qualified customer means. An example of a simple approach is that a prospective customer will qualify if he has a need, a budget and a realistic time frame to get the project completed.

Simply needing or wanting a home repair or improvement is not enough. Many prospects want things they can't afford, or have unrealistic budgets. In order to determine if the customer can afford your services, make sure that he has set a budget sufficient to accomplish the proposed project.

Customers also need to have a realistic time frame for when they want the project done. A prospect who can't tell you when he wants the project completed isn't serious about starting it in the first place.

Asking open-ended questions, those that require more than a one word or yes/no reply, will help in the process of eliciting the information you need. A closed-ended question is one that typically has a one-word response. For example: Do you like this shade of green? --The likely response is either yes or no.

Try asking questions such as the ones outlined below

- What is your end goal for this project?
- What would you like your (bathroom, kitchen, basement, deck, bedroom…) to look like when it is complete?

- Have you seen other examples that you like? You may have seen something in a magazine or in a friend or neighbor's home that you like.

Here are sample questions to help you determine if your prospect has a sufficient budget:

- What is you budget range for this project?
- What (colors, brand, model, style, etc.) have you selected for this part of the project?
- Are you planning on paying for this project all at once, or will you be financing it?

These sample questions can help you determine the prospect's time frame and readiness to start project:

- Can I see your paint color samples?
- What ideas do you really like?
- How soon do you want this project completed?
- What (colors, brand, model, style, etc.) have you selected for this part of the project?

The responses to these questions will give you a better understanding of your prospect's wants and needs, and the information to qualify your prospective customers.

Selling Your Services

How well you present yourself and your business, and the value you bring for the price you are charging are the factors that will determine if you are hired! It is equally important to build initial trust and rapport - to create connection and commonality with someone. The questions you ask prospective customers during the qualifying process can also help you find some common ground to build a connection and relationship. Your prospective customer wants to like and trust you before he can buy something from you. This is not to say that you will become life-long friends, but having rapport means you like talking to and being around someone in a buyer/seller business relationship. Remember, most people want to be active and engaged buyers - they don't want to passively be sold something, they want to take the initiative and actively buy something. People generally prefer to buy from someone they like, with whom they can develop a positive business relationship.

Providing an estimate to a customer is an important part of the selling process, which, if done well, can result in having a customer hire your business for his project. Pricing and estimating jobs is covered in more depth in the Operations section.

If you have done a great job at marketing, qualifying, and rapport building, this will often lead directly to selling. Prospective customers will likely hire you if you meet certain key criteria. What do customers typically want from a home improvement company?

- A company or individual with a good reputation, preferably from a third-party referral.

- Workers who are knowledgeable and expert in what they are doing and can communicate that information in layman's terms.
- People who are easy to reach by phone or email and who are flexible and easy to work with.
- Customers want to feel they are getting a good value and being charged a reasonable price. No one wants to pay too much for any service!
- A quality end product that looks great, functions as intended and will last its typical lifetime.

If you can provide this entire package for your business, then you will be successful at selling your services.

Free & Low-Cost Advertising Strategies
There are many advertising opportunities that will cost you little or nothing. These promotional strategies can help publicize your handyman business while allowing you to save on advertising expenses. Here are some examples:

Materials
- Print flyers advertising your business with tear-off strips at the bottom that include your contact information, and post them on community billboards.

- Make up business cards and be sure to carry them with you wherever you go. Online printers such as VistaPrint (www.vistaprint.com) offer free or low-cost business cards and other business materials. Office supply stores such as Staples (www.staples.com) are also economical. You can quickly and cheaply print your own cards (see the "Business Cards - A DIY Approach" page 49 in this guide).

- Make neighborhood flyers (see Neighborhood Flyers example, page 46). After completing a job, you can leave flyers around the neighborhood or your latest jobsite.

- Use your car, truck, or van as a rolling billboard. You can buy customized signs or lettering to attach to your vehicle.

Referrals
- One of your best sources of new business is referrals from existing clients. Make sure you are in contact with your clients on a regular basis and ask them for referrals. If they like your work, they'll be

happy to share their experiences with their friends, family, colleagues, or neighbors.

- With permission from your customers, place a yard sign at each of your jobsites to promote your company to neighbors.

- Locate a local concierge service and ask to be on their list of services. Concierge services help find various goods and services for their clients. Larger corporations sometimes offer this service as a benefit to their employees.

- Introduce yourself to area real estate agents. Realtors are a great source for referrals. Seller's agents often need to make repairs to get properties ready to sell. Buyer's agents often have clients who need to make improvements once they purchase a property. Just open the phone book and start calling.

- Call property management companies. They manage rental properties and often need to make numerous repairs when turning over properties between tenants or getting new properties ready to be listed for rent.

- Introduce yourself to area home cleaning services. Cleaning services are another excellent source of referrals.

- Contact insurance companies to get on their lists of approved vendors to provide repairs for insurance claims.

Use your Networks
- Call or email all of your family, friends, past co-workers and acquaintances and tell them about your business. Many people like to help out a friend in a new endeavor. (Also see section on "Getting New Clients via Networking," page 39.)

Give Back to Gain Customers
- Volunteer your services at local religious, civic and non-profit organizations in exchange for free advertising in their publications.

- Advertise with local senior citizen resource and referral agencies or senior centers. Offer a discount to seniors in your area.

- Offer a certificate for a FREE hour of service as an auction item for a local non-profit organization's auction fundraiser.

Using the Internet
- It is important for your business to have a presence on the Internet, even if it is a simple one-page website. If you don't have the skills or knowledge to create a website yourself, you might enlist the help of a local college student (or even high school student) to build a website for you. Many students are highly skilled. The student gets some practical experience and you get a basic website.

- Use your email auto signature to promote your business. Create a signature that includes your name, telephone number, company name, and company website URL at the bottom of each email. In some email programs, you can include a logo.

- Try using a free or low-cost service like www.vflyer.com or www.widgetbox.com to make your online advertisement stand out. There are many providers like these that allow you, with little technical expertise, to develop eye-catching advertisements that you can post in online classifieds and marketplaces.

- Ask your customers to join a customer review site and write a review about their positive experiences with you and your company. These include: www.angieslist.com, www.citysearch.com, www.measuredup.com, www.local.yahoo.com, and www.yelp.com

- Many social networking sites like www.facebook.com, www.myspace.com allow businesses to post a free profile.

- Advertise in online marketplaces such as www.craigslist.com or www.backpage.com, which post free business advertisements. A list of free/low cost places to advertise online is included at the end of this section (page 35).

Sharing Your Expertise
- Write home-improvement articles and encourage your local newspaper to publish them. Also publish your articles on a free web log or "blog" (see www.wordpress.com and www.blogger.com).

- Create or share a video on a home improvement tip and post it for free on www.youtube.com. You can also share tips and develop a following on www.twitter.com.

- Call your local newspaper, TV and radio stations. Ask to speak with reporters (local business, real estate, etc.) and volunteer your time and expertise to be interviewed for any home improvement-related story they may be featuring. Suggest story ideas if they were not planning such a feature.

Opportunity in your Community

- Post flyers/business cards at your local hardware store, paint store or home improvement center.

- Publish an ad in the bulletins of your local religious, civic, and non-profit organizations. These are normally low-cost. Also ask if they have advertising sections on their web sites.

- Post ads at common areas for local neighborhood or homeowner's associations (HOA), Mother's clubs, and other similar organizations in your area. Ask your customers to post your business cards or flyers at their clubs or.

- Post free ads on back pages of local weekly newspaper or small low-cost ads in the newspaper classifieds section. Many areas have "Penny Savers" or other shopping-oriented publications.

The following is a list of free/low cost advertising opportunities available on the Internet:

www.angieslist.com
www.areaguides.com
www.backpage.com
www.backyardamerica.com
www.bestwayclassifieds.com
www.bizhwy.com
www.builderstep.com
www.constructionwork.com
www.contractorgallery.com
www.contractorrolodex.com
www.craigslist.com
www.dmoz.org
www.findaho.com
www.getfave.com
www.google.com
www.handyamerican.com
www.hellometro.com
www.hotfrog.com
www.inlocal.com
www.insiderpages.com
www.kijiji.com
www.laborfair.com
www.linkreferral.com
www.local.com
www.localwin.com
www.magicyellow.com
www.merchantcircle.com
www.servicetrades.com
www.stumblehere.com
www.superpages.com
www.toolmandepot.com
www.whatcontractor.net
www.yahoo.com
www.yellowpages.com

www.yelp.com
www.yourcontractordirect.com

Strategies for Cost-Effective Paid Advertising
There are many options for purchasing ads, from newspapers to magazines to television. In order to maximize your advertising dollars, it is important to ask prospective customers how they found you, so you can determine what forms of advertising are most likely to bring in clients. Some paid advertising strategies include:

- Cable and network television
- Radio
- Yellow pages or other telephone directories
- Direct mail
- Coupon mailer packs
- Postcard mailers
- Newspaper and classifieds ads

- Paid Internet advertising (pay per click or impression), such as:
  - www.bing.com
  - www.citysearch.com
  - www.google.com
  - www.yahoo.com
  - www.yodle.com

- Handyman lead and referral services such as:
  - www.bidclerk.com
  - www.contractor.com
  - www.reliableremodeler.com
  - www.renovationexperts.com
  - www.repairs.com
  - www.servicemagic.com

Before you start paying for advertising, try a number of the free options outlined above. Again, be sure to evaluate each advertising option you choose to see what kind of benefit you get from it. In other words, if you pay $1,000 for a print advertisement and it only brings in $100 worth of business, then it was not a successful strategy.

Be sure that there is some way of quantifying what new business results from the specific form of advertising you use. The business that results from each strategy is referred to as ROI, or Return On Investment. For example, if you do a postcard mailing, you can include a special code word or number that customers need to give you to redeem the card. Keep track of which customers use that particular code, and you will be able to determine what new business came from that particular promotion (your return). Then you can compare it with how much you spent on that advertising strategy (your investment).

Getting New Clients via Networking

Networking is one of the simplest and most effective strategies for increasing your customer base. What is networking? Simply introducing yourself and becoming acquainted with new people, and keeping in touch with the people you know. Even if you meet people who may not need your services immediately, they may need you in the future or may know of someone else who needs exactly what you do.

To get started, sit down with a pen and pad and write the numbers 1 through 100 on the left margin. Next, write down the names of 100 people you know in your local area. After you have made your list, contact each person by telephone, letter, or email, let them know about your business, and ask for their assistance by telling their friends, family, and neighbors about your services.

Here are some suggestions to get you started. You may be surprised to find how many people you know!

- Accountant
- Banker
- Barber
- Business club members
- Bowling league members
- Chamber of commerce members
- Clergy
- Club members
- Dentist
- Doctor
- Electrician
- General contractor
- Family members
- Fellow church members

- Financial advisor
- Former classmates
- Friends
- Friends of your spouse/significant other
- HVAC repair person
- Insurance agent
- Lawyer
- Librarian
- Local politicians
- Mechanic
- Mortgage broker
- Neighbors (past and present)
- Newspaper carrier
- Past teachers/instructors
- Plumber
- Pool league members
- Poker/bridge club members
- Professional association members
- Social acquaintances
- Stockbroker
- Your children's teacher(s)
- Other families at your children's school

It is especially important to get out and network in your community when you are first starting out. Whenever you go out, be sure to have plenty of business cards with you. Also, when you go to a party or other social event, see how many new people you can meet. Here are some potential places to network:

- Amusement parks
- Art classes
- Baby showers

- Bowling alleys
- Business networking functions
- Business leads groups or clubs
- Chamber of Commerce meetings
- City parks
- Coffee shops
- Conferences
- Cooking classes
- County fairs
- Dry cleaners
- Family reunions
- Flea markets
- Garage sales
- Golf courses
- Golf driving ranges
- Grocery stores
- High school/college reunions
- Hiking trails
- Home improvement stores
- Kiwanis or other civic club meetings
- Libraries
- Lunch counters
- Movie theaters
- Parties
- Political events
- Public parks
- Pubs and taverns
- Religious events
- Restaurants
- Rotary club meetings
- School events
- Seminars
- Social clubs
- Theatres

- Toastmasters club meetings
- Trade shows
- Vacation destinations
- Yard sales
- Wedding showers
- Weddings
- Workshops

Good luck with networking. It is not easy for some people to do at first, but it will likely be one of the best ways in which to get new clients for your growing handyman business. And, like any other skill, you get better the more you practice

What Customers Really Want

The handyman/home improvement business is, above all, a customer service business. Remember that each customer is different, and will have different needs and wants. Demonstrating that you are trying to accommodate each customer will benefit both you and your customer.

The following is a list of what most customers are looking for in hiring a handyman service:

Punctuality. If you say you are going to arrive at the job site at 9:30 a.m., be there by 9:25 a.m. If you are unavoidably delayed due to traffic or other circumstances, call immediately and let your customer know. I can't emphasize this point enough. It is often the downfall of handyman and other home service businesses.

Cleanliness. After you finish your project, clean up after yourself. A broom and dustpan, sponge, paper towels, and shop-vac are just as important as your other tools. If you had to move furniture or other items to complete your project, put them back in place.

Courtesy. If someone leaves you a voice message or email, make a habit of responding within one business day. Customers, like all of us, appreciate prompt and courteous responses.

Honesty. If you don't know how to do a project or can't answer a question, then say so upfront. Customers will appreciate your honesty, and you may end up saving time and money for both yourself and the customer.

Value. It is critical for customers to feel that you offer good value and good service for the price you charge.

Options. There may be a number of different ways to accomplish a repair or improvement. Inform your customers about their available options and prices.

Opinions. If a customer asks your opinion on something, offer it honestly. You can always say something like, "This may not be my favorite paint color, but I am not the one who will be enjoying the room once it's painted."

Expert knowledge. Customers are turning to you for your knowledge and experience. Think about the big picture of this job. Most customers will appreciate your analyzing and recommending options that will work for the long-term and not simply address the simple task at hand.

Up-front pricing. Customers want to know what a project will cost them before you start. Offer accurate estimates. If you suspect there are potential extra costs, explain them to the customer before you start the project. Avoiding surprises is important. If a problem arises after a job begins, immediately let the customer know and explain the situation and your solution, including the additional cost and length of time it will take to complete.

Communication. The importance of good communication cannot be stressed enough. Keeping customers informed and updated and promptly replying to their questions (without giving a lot of unnecessary information or opinions) can head off future problems and misunderstandings.

Quality. Customers want the end product to function as intended, look good, and last. It is important for a contractor to manage the customer's expectations throughout the transaction. Remember that quality is in eye of the beholder, so if the customer is not satisfied with the quality of the product, you have not finished the job.

Neighborhood Flyer Example

You can print copies and distribute in neighborhoods where you are working. This is also available online as a customizable template. See page 61.

ABC Handyman

<Insert Logo Here>

Hello,

I was in the neighborhood and just completed a project for your neighbor

_____ **at**

_____.

Do you have any small projects around the house that you've been putting off because you have neither the time nor expertise to do them? Give me a call, I'd like to see if I can help. Please call me at 111-111-1111 or email me at abc@abchandyman.com

Have a great day!

Letterhead Example

It is important to present a professional appearance when corresponding with customers. Creating a company logo for your letterhead helps you to establish an identity and build legitimacy for your business. Below is an example of letterhead. This is also available online as a customizable template. See page 61.

Home Improvement Company Name

Company Logo

Address
City, State Zip
Telephone
Fax
Email
Website

November 25, 2009

Dear Ms. or Mr.:

Sincerely,

Referral Request—Example Letter

Use this as an example of a letter to send to previous customers to ask them to refer you and your company to other potential customers. This is also available online as a customizable template. See page 61.

<Insert Company Logo Here>

Name of Company
Address:
Phone:
Fax:
Email:
Website:

Date

Dear_____,

I am trying to build my business through referrals and I want to ask for your assistance. Enclosed please find a few of my new business cards. I would appreciate if you would pass them out to friends and colleagues that you think may benefit from my services. Also, be sure you tell them to reference yourself when they call me so I know who to thank. If you need more cards or need any work done at your own home please let me know.

Sincerely,

Your Home Improvement Specialist

Business Cards - A DIY Approach

Another low-cost alternative to getting business cards printed is to do it yourself with your home computer and printer. Visit your local office supply store and purchase business card blanks. Avery models 5371, 8371, and 8871 work well for these applications.

You can print out your own cards using Microsoft Word. They supply templates for the card blanks. You can also print out templates from Avery:
www.avery.com/avery/en_us/

Go to the Microsoft website: www.microsoft.com, and select the correct template for your business card. Download the file and fill in your contact information, logo, etc. You can print the cards and start handing them out immediately to promote your business.

The following are some business card examples from Microsoft that may work well for your business:

http://office.microsoft.com/en-us/templates/TC062071751033.aspx

http://office.microsoft.com/en-us/templates/TC062071821033.aspx

http://office.microsoft.com/en-us/templates/TC062071621033.aspx

Marketing Letter to a Customer

The following marketing letter can be sent via regular mail or email, and serves as a follow-up to customers that you haven't heard from in several months. This is also available online as a customizable template. See page 61.

Dear (customer name):

We appreciate being able to serve your home improvement needs. I haven't heard from you in a while and just wanted to send a note to see if you had any spring projects that you need our assistance with. Spring is a great time to tackle the following projects:

- Repair broken windows and screens
- Power wash the exterior
- Painting both interior and exterior
- Clear gutters
- Replace worn siding
- And more...

You can reach me at <insert telephone number> or via email <insert email address>. Thank you for your business!

Best wishes,

Your Home Improvement Specialist

Marketing Letter to a Prospective Customer
The following marketing letter can be sent via regular mail or email as a follow-up to prospective customers who you have had contact with but have not yet hired you for any work. This is also available online as a customizable template. See page 61.

Dear (prospective customer name):

Thank you for contacting me in the past regarding your home improvement needs. I wanted to follow-up with you to see if you had any projects that I can assist you with this summer. My expertise is handling projects such as:

- Carpentry
- Wall repair
- Power-washing
- Painting
- Cleaning gutters
- Small fixit items
- And more...

You can reach me at <insert telephone number> or via email <insert email address>.

Best wishes,

Your Prospective Home Improvement Specialist!

Flyer Coupon

Use this as an example to post on your local community bulletin boards. This is also available online as a customizable template. See page 61.

Handyman Company

<INSERT COMPANY LOGO>

Handyman Company provides home maintenance, repair, & improvement services for busy homeowners.
-Licensed
-Insured
-Reliable
-References

Contact us at **TELEPHONE NUMBER**

Email:

Web Page:

$10 Off
Labor on any project over $100

Not valid with other offers. Present at time of estimate.
Expires x/x/xx Code: xxx

$20 Off
Labor on any project over $200

Not valid with other offers. Present at time of estimate.
Expires x/x/xx Code: xxx

Web Advertisement in HTML

Many online free classified advertising websites such as www.craigslist.com and www.backpage.com offer users a way to 'spruce up' their advertisements with the use of basic HTML. HTML stands for "hypertext markup language" and is the software language web browsers use to make the web pages you see on the Internet. Using HTML to make colorful and engaging advertisements on free classified websites will certainly set you apart from other businesses that just use text ads.

The sample HTML ad below is available as one of the free templates available online on page XX. If you prefer, there is information following the template on how you can learn some basic HTML and create your own web ad.

Using the template will allow you to 'copy and paste' rather than having to re-type the text. You will ensure no typing errors when you 'copy and paste,' as HTML is sensitive and won't work correctly if not entered precisely as shown.

You don't need to be a software programmer to develop an attractive web advertisement if you use this template.

A high-quality web advertisement will set you apart from your competitors and present a more professional look to prospective customers. No software skills are required. You simply need to know how to 'cut and paste' on your computer.

Just follow the seven steps below.

Step One:
Download the template titled, "Sample Web Advertisement in HTML". This is available online as a customizable template. See page 61.

Step Two:
Open the "Sample Web Advertisement in HTML" file in your web browser (Internet Explorer, FireFox, Safari etc.)

Step Three:
Go to **File** and select **Edit with Notepad** (or you may edit in another HTML editor).

Step Four:
Using Notepad, you will need to update the text that is UNDERLINED below with your specific company information. Do not change any of the other characters, punctuation, or spacing as this may change the HTML and the page will not view correctly.

You may also type the following text into Notepad (or other html editor).

```
<html>
<b><center>Handyman Services provides home maintenance
and repair services for busy homeowners. <p>
<ul>
<li>Licensed and insured.
<p>
<li>Evening and weekend hours available.
<p>
<li>Great references.
</ul> <p>
Call INSERT TELEPHONE or email <a
href="mailto:INSERT@EMAIL">INSERT EMAIL</a>  <p>
Visit us online at <a
href="http://www.insertweburl.com/">www.insertweburl.com/</
a>  </b> <p>
<a
href="http://www.buildhandymanbusiness.com/">BuildHandym
anBusiness.com   Copyright © 2010</a></center>
</html>
```

Remember - 'copying and pasting the text from the online template will help you to avoid typographical errors.

Step Five:
In Notepad go to **File**, select **Save,** and close Notepad.

Step Six:
Now you can either **Refresh** your browser or close and reopen the "Sample Web Advertisement" file to view your changes.

Step Seven:
Copy and paste the HTML from Notepad or other HTML editor into online advertising (like Craigslist.com). You can also upload it to your own website.

Designing your own Web Advertisement
The Internet is full of free information on how to make basic websites and use HTML. Some tutorials on how to learn basic HTML include:

www.activejump.com
www.htmlgoodies.com
www.pagetutor.com
www.w3schools.com

Once you have learned some basic HTML, you will need a way to write and edit your HTML. There are a number of free HTML editors available to download, such as:

www.html-kit.com
www.notetab.com
www.seamonkey-project.org
www.trellian.com/webpage

Branding Your Business

Branding is simply your company's identity. It includes your company name, logo, letterhead, slogans and taglines, and generally how you present your company in the marketplace. Your brand tells prospective customers who you are and what you are all about. Major corporations spend millions to develop and promote their brands so they become household names. A solid brand is synonymous with a strong company. Start developing your brand by creating your company name and developing your company logo.

There is much written on the subject of branding, and those new to the topic are encouraged to learn all they can to help build their business brand.

Section Summary — Marketing and Sales
Building Your Successful Handyman Business

This section covered promoting, marketing, and selling your services to customers.

- Marketing and sales ends where your quality service begins.
- The main goal of marketing is to attract customers and sell them your services.
- Having specific sales strategies and measuring your advertising results will help you be more effective in marketing your business.
- Quality and customer service will ensure that customers keep coming back and that they refer your business to others.
- A steady stream of qualified customers is key to ensuring success in your home improvement business.

Free Templates and Forms

All businesses, especially new ones, need forms and processes to be organized and successful. Businesses may develop their own, purchase them from other sources, or use the forms provided as part of this guide. If you are borrowing this book from a library, friend, family or colleague, you will need to purchase the guide yourself to access these valuable forms and templates.

There are over 60 templates and forms, which are provided primarily as Microsoft Word, Microsoft Excel, and Rich Text documents. These are customizable for your particular business needs and are provided at no additional charge to the purchasers of this guide.

To access these forms and templates, please register online at: www.buildhandymanbusiness.com/register

Operations

Go confidently in the direction of your dreams. Live the life you have imagined. - Henry David Thoreau

Operations

Business operations are a set of processes that are used to run your company. Operations are where successful marketing and sales efforts end and delivering quality service begins.

The three primary goals of operations are to:
- Promote repeat customers
- Minimize expenses
- Maximize profits

Operations are how you serve your customer, and the quality of service you provide. Having specific systems or processes in place can help you be more efficient. They can help save time AND money so you can increase your sales and serve more customers.

Here are some questions to help you get started thinking about operations:

- What services do you offer?
- When are you available to provide these services? (i.e., days, hours)
- Where do you deliver the services you offer (i.e. geographic service area)
- How are the services are performed? (i.e., by you, your staff, subcontractors)
- How and when do customers pay?

One way of mapping out your operations is to develop a written Standard Operating Procedures manual (SOP). This can be especially helpful if there are multiple people working in the business, so procedures and policies are clear to all employees. When you have written Standard Operating Procedures, it is easier to analyze what you do and how you do it so you can continually refine your procedures to improve efficiency.

Start by writing down every step you take from when a customer hires you, all the way through the job to collecting payment. A sample set of operational steps follows:

1. Customer contacts your business.

2. Estimate provided to customer.

3. Customer accepts estimate and hires you to perform work.

4. Contract is signed.

5. Project is scheduled

6. Deposit payment is collected if needed.

7. Materials are ordered/purchased/delivered.

8. Project work begins.

9. Project is completed.

10. Is customer satisfied, yes or no? If yes, skip to step 12.

11. Customer is contacted and concerns are addressed.

12. Invoice is provided to customer.

13. Payment is received from customer.

14. Customer is added to database.

15. Customer will receive ongoing communication (email, mail, telephone) to solicit new projects and referrals.

Remember, the three main goals of operations are to:
- Promote repeat customers
- Minimize expenses
- Maximize profits

By documenting your operations, you can make adjustments when needed and ensure a smooth, timely, and cost-effective process for you and your customers.

Introduction to Pricing and Estimating Jobs

Pricing

There are several options for pricing your work. Two methods for pricing jobs will be outlined here.

They are:
- Time & materials
- Project-based (or flat rate)

When using Time & Materials pricing (especially useful for small jobs), the contractor will state an hourly rate of pay and the estimated number of hours the task will require to the customer. Any materials provided are priced separately, in addition to the labor.

Project-based pricing includes a flat-rate amount for the labor and an additional cost amount for materials. Determine how many hours the job will take and multiply it by your hourly rate.

Whichever pricing method is used, it is important to correctly estimate the time it will take to complete the job.

To help determine your hourly rate, conduct research on what other home improvement companies and handyman services charge in your area. Assume homeowners are already checking prices of other companies when they contact you. Learning what competitors in your area are charging will greatly assist you in pricing yourself competitively. Take into account your experience, training, special skills, etc.

When you are not hired for projects that you have bid on, it is important to learn why. Ask potential customers why they selected a competitor to learn if pricing was a factor in their decision. Other feedback on your approach and presentation from prospects who did not hire you can also be useful in improving your strategies in the future.

Resources for Writing Estimates

Examples of how to format written estimate for clients and prospective clients are available in this section. You can also find estimate forms at office supply stores.

- Microsoft offers an Excel spreadsheet example for estimating a bathroom renovation. It is downloadable at no cost at http://office.microsoft.com/en-us/templates/TC010186501033.aspx

- Microsoft offers a Word example for estimating a service job. It is downloadable for free at http://office.microsoft.com/en-us/templates/TC060827811033.aspx?pid=CT10143 8791033

- There is also a Project Bid letter example in Microsoft Word, downloadable for free at: http://office.microsoft.com/en-us/templates/TC010185461033.aspx

- Sherwin-Williams offers a free downloadable estimate in PDF format. Register at www.paintersadvantage.com

Estimate Example

Use this as a guide to develop your own estimates. This is also available online as a customizable template. See page 61.

\<Insert Name\>
Estimate

\<Insert Company Address\>   **DATE:**
\<Insert Telephone\>
\<Insert Email\>

Bill To: **For:**

DESCRIPTION	ESTIMATED AMOUNT
Labor:	
Materials:	
Exclusion (s):	
Estimated TOTAL	

Scheduling Jobs

Once you have been awarded the job, scheduling the job and keeping track of your time can be a challenge in itself. It is important to use a calendar or scheduling system to keep on track. Some people use a notebook or a paper calendar. Others will keep track on their computers or handheld electronic calendars. There are many calendaring and scheduling resources available to you, and some are low-cost or free. Take advantage of these resources as you develop your business.

Google has a free online calendar system: (www.google.com/calendar).
Yahoo also has a similar free calendar at www.calendar.yahoo.com.

There are other systems available for free or a low monthly cost (Intuit the makers of QuickBooks accounting software has a fee-based online calendar and customer tracking system see www.customermanager.com). The limitation of online calendars is that you need to be connected to the Internet to view or add new events or update existing ones. One remedy for this is to regularly print out a paper copy of your calendar and make notes on it when you are in the field. Once you are back at your computer, update your schedule online.

Many contractors use handheld PDAs (Personal Data Assistants) or the newer smart phones. The prices for these have significantly dropped in recent years. The functions of a PDA, such as calendars, address books, and email, are now available on many of the smart phones. Having a PDA or smart phone allows you to update while you are away from your computer, and to synch your calendar on the PDA or smart phone with the calendar on your computer.

Paper calendars, Daytimers, Filofaxs, weekly planners, desk calendars, wall calendars, and plain old paper and pencil are also good choices, as these can come along wherever you go and are not subject to electric or connection problems. Using pencil is often more practical, as it is easy to update or amend projects.

Find a system for keeping track of your jobs that works best for you. The more organized you are, the smoother your operations will be. A sample weekly schedule follows.

Weekly Work Schedule

Use this as an example to keep track of your weekly schedule. Planning ahead often saves time in the long run. This is also available online as a customizable template. See page 61.

Weekly Work Schedule for week of _____

	Mon	Tues	Wed	Thur	Fri	Sat	Sun
7:00AM							
7:30AM							
8:00AM							
8:30AM							
9:00AM							
9:30AM							
10:00AM							
10:30AM							
11:00AM							
11:30AM							
12:00PM							
12:30PM							
1:00PM							
1:30PM							
2:00PM							
2:30PM							
3:00PM							
3:30PM							
4:00PM							
4:30PM							
5:00PM							
5:30PM							
6:00PM							
6:30PM							

Prospective Customer – Tracking Sheet

You will need a way to keep track of prospective customers that contact you to inquire about your services. There are many commercially available software programs that help with this task. You can use this document to track prospective clients. Once you they have hired you, transfer their information to the Client Tracking Sheet. This is also available online as a customizable template. See page 61.

Prospective Client-Tracking Sheet

Date	Name	Tel.	Address	How did they find you?	Services Required

Helpful Resources

There are an abundance of resources available to you, mostly free of charge. Take advantage of these resources as you develop your business.

Many home improvement stores offer free clinics to learn new skills. Technical and community colleges offer training programs in a number of different trades. Your local public library will also have many free resources available to you.

The following is an alphabetical list of some of the free online resources that may be helpful for starting or growing your handyman business.

www.acehardware.com
www.benjaminmoore.com
www.bobvila.com
www.contractortalk.com
www.diychatroom.com
www.diynetwork.com
www.epa.gov/lead/pubs/renovation.htm
www.hammerzone.com
www.handymanclub.com
www.hgtv.com
www.homedepot.com
www.hometips.com
www.housefixer.info
http://forums.craigslist.org/?forumID=64
www.jchs.harvard.edu
www.jlconline.com
www.lowes.com
www.michaelholigan.com
www.nahb.org

www.nari.org
www.naturalhandyman.com
www.onthehouse.com
www.pdca.org
www.qualifiedremodeler.com
www.rd.com/familyhandyman
www.sherwin-williams.com
www.thisoldhouse.com
www.tipking.com
www.toolbase.org
www.truevalue.com
www.weekendhandyman.com

Customer Tracking Sheet

This is a form you can use to keep track of current customers. This is also available online as a customizable template. See page 61.

Client Tracking Sheet					
Name	Tel.	Email	Address	Work Performed	Follow-up Required

What Tools and Supplies Do I Need To Get Started?

Chances are that you may already have many of the tools and equipment that you need. Basic hand tools, a computer, and a vehicle are all you really need to get started. As your business grows or as new projects call for additional tools, you may purchase them as needed.

A Tool Inventory Tracking List is included in the free templates (See page 61). Consider having these helpful tools and supplies on hand:

- Broom and dustpan
- Caulking for baths
- Caulking for painting
- Chalk line
- Chisel
- Clamps
- Cordless Drill
- Drill bits
- Dry wall spackle
- Drywall repair tools
- Duct tape
- Extension cord
- File
- First aid kit
- Flashlight
- Garbage bags
- Hammer
- Hand cleaners
- Hatchet/axe
- Ladder
- Level
- Maps of your service area
- Masking tape
- Nails, assorted

- Nail set
- Note pad and pencil
- Paint brushes
- Paint drop clothes
- Paint pan
- Paint, primer
- Paint rollers
- Pen, pencil & paper
- Personal computer or laptop
- PDA or Smart Phone
- Plane
- Pliers
  - Channel lock pliers
  - Electrician's pliers
  - Needle nose pliers
  -
- Pry bar
- Rasp
- Rubber mallet
- Sand paper or sanding block
- Saw horses
- Saws
  - Carpenters saw
  - Chop saw
  - Circular saw
  - Coping Saw
  - Hack saw
  - Hand saw
  - Jig saw
  - Miter saw
  - Reciprocating saw
  - Table saw
- Screw driver set
- Screws, assorted
- Shop vacuum

- Spackling knife
- Square
- Staple gun
- Step ladder
- Stud finder
- Tape measure
- Tile setting tools
- Tool bag/tool box
- Tool belt
- Utility knife
- Vise grips
- Wood glue
- Wrenches
  - Adjustable wrench
  - Allen wrench set
  - Socket wrench set

Vendor Contact Information Sheet Example
Use this example as a method to keep track of your vendors and suppliers. This is also available online as a customizable template. See page 61.

| Vendor Contact Information Sheet | | | | | |
Name	Tel.	Email	Address	Services/ Products	Notes

Fax Cover Sheet

Use this example cover sheet when faxing estimates or other documents. This is also available online as a customizable template. See page 61.

<Insert Logo Here>

Name of Home Improvement Company

Address:
Phone:
Fax:
Email:
Website:

FAX COVER

TO:

FROM:

DATE:

Number of pages including cover: _____

Message:

Jobs To Avoid

Sometimes you may come across prospective customers that have projects that you should not take on. Here are a few guidelines on jobs to avoid.

- Jobs requiring a licensed individual to perform the needed services (e.g. plumber, electrician, general contractor, asbestos abatement, lead abatement, mold abatement, HVAC, EPA RRP Certified Renovator etc.)

- Jobs without clear objectives outlined by the prospective customer.

- Projects that involve performing tasks that you have little to no experience with and that go beyond your skill level.

- Jobs that are very labor-intensive or are hazardous to your health and require special licensing, such as working with lead paint, asbestos, mold, high voltage, high heights etc.

- Jobs correcting sub-par work done by homeowner do-it-yourselfers, or correcting sub-par work done by other contractors.

- A job where the prospective customer is extremely difficult to meet with, either in person or over the telephone, to clarify his project expectations. If a customer is difficult to communicate with and unavailable prior to the job, the situation is not likely to improve during the project.

A word about difficult customers: You can try to please all of the customers all of the time but if you make it to 90% of the time you are doing well! Some customers just can't be pleased no matter how hard you try. When you identify this type of customer, try to come to a project completion and move on. Remember, a 90% customer satisfaction rating is excellent and what you should strive for.

Getting Paid

Many contractors fail to run a successful business because of poor cash flow management, so it is important to make sure you are getting paid and making a profit. "Cash flow management" means monitoring the money coming into your business and the money going out of your business.

Your agreement with your customer should explicitly state how and when you will get paid (see also Contracts and Customer Terms, page 93). It is wise to get deposits for larger projects and to pay for needed materials. If materials need to be special-ordered ahead of time, it is best to get a deposit in full, especially if items are not returnable. If you are working on a large project, getting a materials deposit up front is key, and then requesting progress payments each week until the project is completed. Getting paid each week gives you and your customer a chance to review progress and smooth out any issues prior to the end of the project.

Cash and checks are acceptable forms of payment. Also consider accepting credit cards as a form of payment for your customer's convenience. Beware of offers you may get in the mail or via email about accepting cards. Often they require purchasing equipment and paying monthly fees.

Consider using online credit card processing services that allow you to email an invoice to your customers that they can pay online with their credit cards. These services typically charge you 2-3% of the total as a fee. They do not charge monthly fees or require you to purchase any equipment. You may absorb the processing fee, or add 2-3% to all of your invoices.

Websites like: www.paypal.com and www.google.com/checkout are two good examples of these online services.

Consider adding the 2-3% credit card processing fee to all invoices and then offer customers a 2-3% discount if they pay by cash or check.

How Much Can You Earn?

How much you earn is really up to you. Your earning potential is proportional to the effort you put into your business. The table below offers an example of how much you can earn if you charge $35 per hour for your services.

# Hours Billed Each Week	Weekly Gross Revenue	Monthly Gross Revenue	Annual Gross Revenue
10	$ 350.00	$ 1,400.00	$ 16,800.00
15	$ 525.00	$ 2,100.00	$ 25,200.00
20	$ 700.00	$ 2,800.00	$ 33,600.00
25	$ 875.00	$ 3,500.00	$ 42,000.00
30	$ 1,050.00	$ 4,200.00	$ 50,400.00
35	$ 1,225.00	$ 4,900.00	$ 58,800.00
40	$ 1,400.00	$ 5,600.00	$ 67,200.00
45	$ 1,575.00	$ 6,300.00	$ 75,600.00
50	$ 1,750.00	$ 7,000.00	$ 84,000.00
55	$ 1,925.00	$ 7,700.00	$ 92,400.00
60	$ 2,100.00	$ 8,400.00	$ 100,800.00

This table offers an example of how much you can earn if you charge $50 per hour rate for your services.

# Hours Billed Each Week	Weekly Gross Revenue	Monthly Gross Revenue	Annual Gross Revenue
10	$ 500.00	$ 2,000.00	$ 24,000.00
15	$ 750.00	$ 3,000.00	$ 36,000.00
20	$ 1000.00	$ 4,000.00	$ 48,000.00
25	$ 1,250.00	$ 5,000.00	$ 60,000.00
30	$ 1,500.00	$ 6,000.00	$ 72,00.00
35	$ 1,750.00	$ 7,0000.00	$ 84,000.00
40	$ 2,000.00	$ 8,000.00	$ 96,000.00
45	$ 2,250.00	$ 9,000.00	$ 108,000.00
50	$ 2,500.00	$ 10,000.00	$ 120,000.00
55	$ 2,750.00	$ 11,000.00	$ 132,000.00
60	$ 3,000.00	$ 12,000.00	$ 144,000.00

Pricing your work correctly and getting paid on time are both important elements to having a successful and profitable business. Learning and practicing these estimating skills can ensure that your business will grow and thrive.

Quality Control

Quality control means ensuring every step of the way that your end product, both materials and service, will be of the best possible quality. Having quality standards in place at the beginning of the job makes it very likely that you won't get called back to repair mistakes or provide warranty service. Customers recognize when you are conscientious and take a quality approach to your work. Taking this extra step often results in being called back for future projects. It also means your customers will refer your services to others, which will lead to even more business.

Customer Satisfaction

Customer satisfaction is making sure that you have happy, satisfied customers. Happy customers call you back to do additional work. They tell their friends, family and colleagues about you, which will likely lead to more business. Unhappy customers don't call you back for additional future work. They do tell their friends, family, and colleagues and spread the word about their unhappy experience with you. This, of course, does not earn you new customers or new business, and can lead to a bad reputation in your community.

There are generally two types of customers: the reasonable and the unreasonable. Thankfully, most customers are in the reasonable category. If customers are not satisfied with some aspect of your service, take the time to listen to them and allow them to express their concerns, then work together toward a mutually satisfactory solution.

There will always be a few unreasonable customers. These individuals won't be happy or satisfied no matter what you say or do. Once you recognize this, it is best to try and resolve the situation as soon as possible and as professionally as possible. You won't be getting additional projects or referrals from this person. The best you can hope for is that your next customer will be a reasonable one!

If customer service is not your strong suit, consider getting some training on how to work with difficult customers.

Successful contractors with many satisfied customers possess the following characteristics:

- Cleanliness
- Courtesy

- Expert knowledge
- Honesty
- Options
- Opinions
- Punctuality
- Upfront Pricing

Contracts and Customer Terms

Stating everything clearly in writing can help you and your client understand your responsibilities and expectations. This may not be necessary or practical for very small jobs, however high-dollar projects should certainly include a contract that delineates everything for both parties.

Sample contracts are available to purchase at office supply stores; you can also find sample contracts online that you can adapt. Another option is to hire a lawyer to write up a standard contract for you, which also has its advantages, especially when dealing with high-dollar projects.

Contracts should include specific language covering:

- Deposits
- Payment schedule
- Scope of work
- Scheduling
- Hazards
- Changes to project
- Dispute management
- Mechanic's liens
- Subcontractor liens
- Typical work procedures
- Contingencies

Consult an attorney for a more comprehensive list and any advice concerning contracts.

Spelling out how and when you get paid is a crucial part of a contract agreement; just as managing your cash flow (money coming in and out of your business) is a crucial part of having a successful business.

A sample basic contract is available online as a customizable template. See page 61.

Computers and Software

Computers can be immensely helpful for timesaving, organizing, and analyzing jobs and business strategies. Computers help us keep track of schedules, communicate with customers, suppliers, and vendors, perform bookkeeping tasks, do necessary research, promote and advertise the business, and much more.

If the computer is a foreign tool to you, take advantage of the many free and low-cost basic computer classes available. Check your library, local community college, or small business center for a schedule of computer classes. The costs of computers and software have come down significantly over the years. Google (see www.Google.com/docs) currently offers free email, word processing and spreadsheet software online.

Here is a list of minimum skills you need to be successful with your business computer:
- Ability to connect to the Internet
- Business email address and ability to send and retrieve emails
- Ability use a basic spreadsheet software application (e.g. MS Excel)
- Ability to use a basic word processing software application (e.g. MS Word)

Section Summary — Operations
Building Your Successful Handyman Business

Operations are where your successful marketing and sales efforts end and delivering your quality service begins.

The main goals of operations are to:
- Promote repeat customers
- Minimize expenses
- Maximize profits for your service business

Operations are how you serve your customer and the quality of service you provide. Having specific systems or processes in place can help you become more efficient. They can help save time so you can increase your sales and serve more customers.

Finance and Administration

The measure of who we are is what we do with what we have -Vince Lombardi

Financial Matters

Keeping track of financial matters is probably the most important aspect of running any business. Without accurate financial systems you will find yourself in hot water with the 'Tax Man' or even out of business! Keeping track of your expenses, revenue, and cash flow is how you determine how well your business is doing. It is the like the game scorecard, and helps you determine the overall heath of your business.

For those without accounting or bookkeeping training or experience, consider taking an introductory accounting class at a local community college. Many small business development organizations also offer educational seminars on basic accounting principles and concepts. Understanding these concepts will be of great help if you ever plan to get a loan to expand your business. You should also consider hiring a CPA (Certified Public Accountant) to help you set up business accounting and bookkeeping systems and monitor your progress.

Business Plan

Would you build a deck or a home addition without having a plan? It is just as important to have a plan in place to build your business. Your business plan can be as simple or as complex as you want it to be. Whether it is produced with fancy software or handwritten in a notebook, it will be the blueprint for building your business. This a document that also should be reviewed, and amended if needed, on a regular basis, at least once per fiscal quarter.

The two most important questions your business plan should answer are:

1. What are your financial goals for the next one to five years?
2. How do you plan on reaching these goals?

A simple business plan outline is provided below. Additionally, you can find free resources and assistance for developing a business plan at the following links:

- Small Business Administration www.sba.gov
- SCORE   www.score.org
- Small Business Development   www.sbdcnet.org

Sample Business Plan Outline

Use the business plan outline below to help develop your own written business plan.

Business Plan for <Name or Business>
Date last updated:

Owner:
Business name:
Address:
Telephone:
E-mail:
Website:

Summary of Business Plan:

Services offered:

Owner's experience:

Goals:
Examples:

- To increase gross annual sales from$75k to $100k in one year.
- To grow customer base from 40 to 80 customers within two years.
- To increase average project size by 10% within one year.
- To expand service area into nearby town within three years.

Company Description:

Mission statement:

Example-Our mission is to provide high-quality home improvement services that are affordably priced.

Form of ownership:
Example: *Sole proprietor/LLC/Corporation/Partnership*

Company Strengths:

Company Challenges:

Service Area:

Services Offered:

Marketing Plan

    Market research:

    Customer Profile:

    List of Competitors:

    Niche: What sets you apart from the competition?

Marketing and Advertising Strategies
-
-
-
-

List of Suppliers/Vendors/Subcontractors:

Managing Accounts Receivable (How will you be paid?):

Managing Accounts Payable (How will you pay others?):

Management and Organization:

Professional and Advisory Support:

Financial Plan

Below you will find examples of a balance sheet and cash flow statement to help you develop your financial plan. If you are unfamiliar with creating a balance sheet or cash flow statement, you may want to take an introductory accounting skills course. Your local community college or small business center may offer free or inexpensive accounting classes.

These forms are also available online as a customizable template. See page 61.

Balance Sheet

Revenues	$
Fixed Costs (minus)	$
Variable Costs (minus)	$
Net Profit/Loss	$

Projected Monthly Cash Flow Statement

Month	1	2	3	4	5	6	7	8	9	10	11	12
Cash In												
Cash Out												
Balance												

Bookkeeping and Record Keeping

Keeping track of your revenue and expenses is key to understanding the financial health of your business. Below you will find Excel spreadsheets, which you can use to track your expenses and revenue. There are several basic computer programs that offer more robust bookkeeping for your small business, such as Quicken: www.quicken.intuit.com and QuickBooks: www.quickbooks.com. QuickBooks also offers a Simple Start version of their accounting software for free: www.quickbooks.intuit.com.

Many community colleges offer classes on how to use software applications, if you are not already familiar with them.

Record keeping can be time consuming for business owners, but it is necessary in order to ensure accurate company books. There are several software packages to you might use to assist with this process. Software applications are great, but you will still need to keep paper receipts and documentation.

A simple record keeping system will cost about $15 to $20. Just follow these easy steps:

> **Step One.** From your local office supply store, buy 24 manila file folders with tabs at the top, and an expanding accordion-style file folder with the months of the year pre-printed on the tabs.

> **Step Two.** On twelve of the file folders write the word "Revenue" on the tab and on the other twelve write "Expenses" on the tab.

Step Three. Place one of each file folder in each month of the folder.

Step Four. You are ready to start! During the month, every time you receive money, place your documentation (copy of invoice, check, etc.) in the 'Revenue' folder.

Step Five. For every expense you incur, place the vendor invoice, cash register receipt or other documentation into the "Expenses" envelope.

Step Six. When it is time to do your quarterly and year-end taxes (more on this topic later), everything you need will be neatly organized and in one place.

Step Seven. At the end of your first year of business, simply remove all the file folders and place them in a large envelope labeled "Revenue and Expenses for Tax Year _____ ". Replace with new file folders in each month at the start of your second and subsequent years.

This simple way of record keeping is a good way to start out and have everything organized and in one place. There are more complex record-keeping systems, such as electronically scanning your documents. Outsourcing your bookkeeping functions may be more suitable as your business develops.

It is advisable to meet with a Certified Public Accountant (CPA) to ensure you are starting out on the right path. This can help you avoid potential problems with the IRS and your state Department of Revenue in the future. You will need to hold on to these records in case you are ever audited. Your accountant will let you know how long you will need to keep these records.

Invoice Example
Use this as a guide to develop your own invoices. This is
also available online as a customizable template. See page
61.

<Insert Company Name>
INVOICE

<Insert Company Address> **DATE:**
<Insert Telephone>
<Insert Email>

Bill To: **For:**

DESCRIPTION	AMOUNT
Labor:	
Materials:	
TOTAL	

Expense Tracking Sheet

Use this as an example to track your business related expenses. This is also available online as a customizable template. See page 61.

Expense Tracking Sheet

Date	Amt	Vendor	Ref. #	Category	Balance
	$				$
	$				$
	$				$
	$				$
	$				$
	$				$
	$				$
	$				$
	$				$
	$				$
	$				$
	$				$
	$				$
	$				$
	$				$
	$				$
	$				$
	$				$
	$				$
	$				$
	$				$
	$				$
	$				$
	$				$
	$				$
	$				$
	$				$
	$				$
	$				$
	$				$

Invoice Tracking Sheet

Use this as a spreadsheet to track the money (revenue) your have earned on each project and to track your invoices.
This is also available online as a customizable template.
See page 61.

Invoice Tracking Sheet

Inv. #	Amt	Customer	Date	Description	Balance
	$				$
	$				$
	$				$
	$				$
	$				$
	$				$
	$				$
	$				$
	$				$
	$				$
	$				$
	$				$
	$				$
	$				$
	$				$
	$				$
	$				$
	$				$
	$				$
	$				$
	$				$
	$				$
	$				$
	$				$
	$				$
	$				$
	$				$

Mileage Journal

Use this document to keep track of mileage driven for business purposes, such as driving to jobs, delivering materials, providing estimates, etc. If you document your mileage, this can be used as a business expense when figuring your taxes. This document is also available online as a customizable template. See page 61.

Mileage Journal

Date	Miles	Purpose

Banking and Credit

It is important to pick the right bank for your business - to cash your payment checks from customers, hold your deposits, and set up a business checking account to pay your vendors and suppliers. Shop around, as many banks offer special accounts geared toward small businesses. Some banks may ask you for information such as a business license and tax identification number prior to setting up your business account.

Establishing business lines of credit with your suppliers is important as you grow your business. When you get that big job, you can purchase supplies on credit and have a month to pay the expense. Most of the Big Box retailers offer basic credit cards to commercial patrons. Having a business credit card is also a good idea, since many offer incentives, including cash back rewards, and you can aggregate all your expenses, which is much easier than having to keep track of multiple cards. Be sure to review and understand the terms and conditions before signing up for any new credit card.

Collections

Over the course of your business, you may run into customers who don't pay their bill or only pay part of the bill, and you will need to collect payment from them. This is a delicate situation, as most service providers want to maintain good relationships with customers, who will call you for future work or refer you to others.

It is best to spell out payment terms ahead of time in writing (see section on Contracts). However, if a customer hasn't sent you a payment by the time specified, it is usually best to contact him or her by telephone. There are a number of reasons why the customer hasn't paid (never received invoice, just plain forgot, was away on vacation, the dog ate it! etc.) In many cases, a gentle reminder can yield prompt payment.

If you call and the customer has an issue or complaint with your work, it is to your benefit to try and resolve it. Ask the customer if there is anything you can do to make him happy so that the situation can be resolved and you can be paid. Offer to come meet with him in person. Often simply listening to the issues and offering to correct a problem is all that's needed. Offering to discount the current invoice is not advisable, especially if you have a written agreement with the customer.

If this effort doesn't yield results, there are a number of additional strategies you can employ. These strategies include:

1. Send a letter demanding payment.
2. Hire an attorney to write and send a letter demanding payment.
3. File a mechanic's lien on their property. An attorney will likely be needed for this.

4. File a complaint in small claims court.
5. Hire a collection agency to collect payment

Of course, once you go down this path you have set up an adversarial relationship. This does not guarantee a payment, but will guarantee losing a customer.

What Kind of Insurance Do I Need?

Insurance is one of those things in life that you pay for in hopes that you never have to use it. To help you determine what kind of insurance you need for your business, start by asking the insurance agent who handles your auto and home insurance. If your agent doesn't handle business insurance, ask him for a referral to an agent who does. A business insurance agent will know any legal requirements for insurance, as well as what options are available to. Each state has its own rules and regulations on what types of insurance may be required for your business.

Below is a basic explanation of the types of insurance you should consider purchasing for your handyman business.

Workers Compensation Insurance: This insurance covers you if you are hurt on the job. Some jobs that you bid on may require you to show proof of this type of insurance before starting the job. This insurance may be required by law in your area.

General Liability Insurance: This insurance covers claims of injury or property damage on the job as a result of actions for which your business is legally liable.

Business Property Insurance: This covers against loss of business property (buildings, equipment, inventory etc.). Check with your agent to see if you may already be covered by your homeowner's or renter's policy.

Business Interruption (loss of income) Insurance: This insurance provides coverage if your business cannot operate due to a natural disaster, accident, or other unforeseen circumstance.

Auto Insurance: Be sure to alert your auto insurance agent that you are using your vehicle for business purposes, to make sure you are completely covered.

Short or Long-term Disability Insurance: A type of insurance that provides income to you if you become disabled and are unable to work.

Errors and Omissions: This provides coverage for mistakes made in performing your service.

Again, it is best to check with your insurance agent to better understand your particular needs. Thoroughly review each of your policies so you know what is and is not included in your coverage.

Government Compliance for Small Business

Setting up a small business can be a daunting task. One important aspect of starting your business is compliance with government regulations. Different levels of government require businesses to submit different forms of paperwork or documentation, such as applications, forms, and vouchers.

The goal of this section is to make the process of government paperwork easier to understand and complete, so that you can concentrate your efforts on other import aspects of starting and running your business. Each section includes the following:

- The name of the form.
- An explanation of the form's purpose and what you have to do to be in compliance with the regulations.
- When you are required to file the form.
- And finally, where you can find the form and more information if you have questions.

Compliance Items Include:
- A. IRS Form SS- 4, Application for EIN
- B. IRS Form 1040-ES, Estimated Tax for Individuals (including Payment Voucher)
- C. IRS Form 1040 Schedule, Profit or Loss From Business
- D. IRS Form 1040 Schedule SE, Self-Employment Tax
- E. State Estimated Income Tax
- F. Privilege License / Business License Application
- G. Certificate of Assumed Name for a Sole Proprietorship
- H. Sales Tax
- I. Insurance

The information in this section is intended for individuals who will be self-employed and will not have employees working for them. Being an employer requires significant additional government paperwork and recordkeeping, and is not covered in this guide. If you are planning to hire employees, there are payroll services that specialize in helping small businesses with the complex tasks of employee payroll. Your accountant should be able to assist you in locating such a service.

Being in compliance with government regulations from the start of your business may not put money in your pocket, but will undoubtedly save you time, energy, heartache and money in the long run.

The federal, state, county, and local governments each have a hand in regulating sole proprietorships (one person having his or her own business with no additional employees). The federal government regulates sole proprietorships through the Internal Revenue Service. Each state regulates through its Department of Revenue. Each county or municipal government may also have a part in regulating sole proprietorships through its Register of Deeds. Finally, each municipal (town or city) government may regulate sole proprietorships through its Business Licensing Division. Each governmental entity has its own specific forms and requirements. Be sure to check with your locality for specific regulations in your jurisdiction.

Some states have specific licenses for those performing home repair and handyman services. Many professions and industries have their own regulatory and licensing requirements, so you may need to check those as well.

FORM NAME:
IRS Form SS- 4 Application for EIN

EXPLANATION:
This is an application form to receive an Employer Identification Number (EIN) also called a Federal Identification Number (FID). The IRS uses this number to identify your business like they use your Social Security number to identify you as an individual. The information you provide establishes your business tax account with the IRS. This number is also sometimes used as an identifier with your bank and with other governmental bodies. After you fill in the form, call the IRS at their toll free number (on the second page of the SS-4 Instructions form) and they will issue you a number over the phone. Keep the completed form for your records. There is no charge to receive this number.

WHEN:
File this form when you establish your business.

WHERE:
File this form online, over the telephone, or it can be mailed to the IRS

This form is available online at this link:
http://www.irs.gov/businesses/small/article/0,,id=102767,00.html

B

FORM NAME:
IRS Form 1040-ES Estimated Tax for Individuals
(including Payment Voucher)

EXPLANATION:
This is the form used to both estimate and pay federal income taxes on income made from your business. These payments are made to the IRS on a quarterly basis. The instructions on Form 1040-ES indicate where to send your payment and voucher. This is dependent upon what state you reside in.

After you make you initial payment, the IRS will send you preprinted forms and envelopes to use for subsequent payments. If you are subject to withholding from another job, you may be able to have your employer increase the amount of withholding and not be subject to this requirement. The IRS can levy penalties for non-payment, underpayment, and late payment of these taxes.

WHEN:
You may pay all of your estimated taxes by April 15 or pay it in four equal installments on or before April 15, June 15, September 15, and January 15. If the 15th of the month falls on a weekend, then you have until the next business day.

WHERE:
This form is located at this link:
http://www.irs.gov/pub/irs-pdf/f1040es.pdf

C

FORM NAME:
IRS Form 1040 Schedule C Profit or Loss From Business

EXPLANATION:
This is the form to report your profit or loss from your sole proprietorship business. It is filed as an attachment to your personal taxes (Form 1040). It is important to keep accurate records and save all business related receipts in order to complete this form.

WHEN:
This form is filed on or before April 15th each year.

WHERE:
This form is available online at this link:
http://www.irs.gov/pub/irs-pdf/f1040sc.pdf

FORM NAME:
IRS Form 1040 Schedule SE Self-Employment Tax

EXPLANATION:
This is the form to report your self-employment taxes for your sole proprietorship business. Self-employment tax is similar to Social Security taxes (FICA and Medicare) that are deducted from an employee's earnings. This form is filed as an attachment to your personal taxes (Form 1040).

WHEN:
This form is filed on or before April 15th each year.

WHERE:

This form is available online at this link:

http://www.irs.gov/pub/irs-pdf/f1040sse.pdf

FORM NAME:
STATE Individual Estimated Income Tax

EXPLANATION:
This is the form used to both estimate and pay state income taxes on income made from your business. This is similar to what you have to do with the federal government with Form 1040-ES. These payments are made to your state Department of Revenue on a quarterly basis. After you make your initial payment, your state will usually send you preprinted forms to use for subsequent payments. Your state can levy penalties for non-payment, underpayment, and late payment of these taxes.

WHEN:
You may pay all of your estimated taxes by April 15 or pay it in four equal installments by April 15, June 15, September 15, and January 15. If the 15th of the month falls on a weekend, then you have until the next business day.

WHERE:
Forms are available at your state's Department of Revenue

FORM NAME:
Privilege License / Business License Application

EXPLANATION:
In most municipalities you will need to secure a business license also called a Privilege License. Most small business owners just starting out are working out of their homes. Some municipalities have special licenses and permits covering home-based businesses. It is best to check with you town/city hall to find out the requirements in your area. There is normally a fee that must be submitted with this application. Some states and municipalities require special licensing for specific industries. It is best to check with your state or local small business administration office for further details.

WHEN:
File this form when you establish your business name.

WHERE:
These are available usually at your County, City or Town Hall.

FORM NAME:
Certificate of Assumed Name for a Sole Proprietorship

EXPLANATION:
The Certificate of Assumed Name for a Sole Proprietorship is sometimes called dba or Doing Business As. You may be required to file this form whenever you use a name other than your given name for business purposes. Prior to submission, contact your local Register of Deeds to ensure the name you plan to use is not already in use by another business. There is usually a small cost to file this form. At some point you may want to incorporate your business and use a corporate name. It is best to speak with a CPA or business attorney to examine the pros and cons of incorporating in your state.

WHEN:
File this form when you establish your business name.

WHERE:
File this form at your local County Court or Register of Deeds office.

NAME:
Sales Tax Collection

EXPLANATION:
If your business buys items and resells them, then states with a sales tax will require you to register with them. This will allow you to purchase items and not pay sales tax on the items yourself, however, you will collect sales tax from your customer at the time of sale. This sales tax revenue is then remitted to a state agency, typically the state Department of Revenue.

WHEN:
Explore when you establish your business or when you plan to start selling products.

WHERE:
State Department of Revenue

I

NAME:
Insurance for your business

EXPLANATION:
Insurance for your business is something you should consider when you are starting your business. Having certain types of insurance such as workers compensation for your business is required in some states. Insurance may come in several types of polices. That may include: workers compensation, general liability, errors and omissions, auto, disability and business interruption to name a few. Having a conversation with your current insurance agent that covers your personal policies is usually a good place to start. Also see previous section titled "What Insurance Do I Need?"

WHEN:
Explore when you establish your business.

WHERE:
Insurance agent or agency.

Section Summary — Finance and Administration
Building Your Successful Handyman Business

This section covered a number of important topics related to starting and operating a successful business.

- A business plan provides you with a framework for directing your business.
- Tracking money coming in and going out allows you to monitor the success and financial health of your business.
- Collecting payments that customers owe is necessary to keep your business successful
- Sufficient insurance coverage is necessary for your business.
- Complying with Government laws and regulations is critical

Conclusion

Congratulations on choosing to read this guide and starting or expanding your handyman/home improvement business! My goal has been to provide you with information to assist you in this endeavor.

Remember - you don't have to re-invent the wheel - "Building Your Successful Handyman Business" has been developed and field-tested by the owner and operator of a success handyman/home improvement company.

Successful contracting businesses do not get that way by only focusing on their trade skills. They are successful because they develop and fine-tune the business side of their enterprise as well. Marketing, operations, financial, and administrative tasks need to be part of your daily business strategy in order for your business to be profitable.

My hope is that you are able to put into practice many of the concepts presented in this guide to help grow your own business.

Best of Luck to you!

CS

Building Your Successful Handyman Business
A guide to starting and operating a profitable business

- Interested in starting your own handyman business?

- Have great trade skills but want to learn more about the business side?

- Need help in growing an existing business?

Answers to these questions and more are found in this guide, *Building Your Successful Handyman Business: A guide to starting and operating a profitable business.* This guide provides real-world, proven strategies to help build a successful and profitable home improvement business. Purchasers of the guide may access over 60 customizable business forms and templates for use in their own business.

Please visit www.buildhandymanbusiness.com

About the Author

Chuck Solomon owns and operates a successful home improvement business serving the Triangle area (Raleigh, Durham, and Chapel Hill) of North Carolina (see www.carolinahandyman.com). Mr. Solomon has been a handyman most of his life, starting at an early age by helping his dad and uncles with home projects. Even as he went to college and graduate school, and worked in the fields of non-profit management, consulting, information technology, and human resources, he continued to perform handyman/home improvement projects for himself and others. This guide is the result of his experience spending many hours starting and growing his own home improvement business. When not fixing things, Mr. Solomon enjoys hiking, kayaking, cooking, traveling and spending time with his family.

Additional Resources:
For additional resources to help build a successful home improvement or handyman business, please visit www.buildhandymanbusiness.com

In addition to this guide, other services are available from the author and include: business coaching and consulting, workshop and seminar presentations. Learn more at www.buildhandymanbusiness.com.

Notes

CPSIA information can be obtained at www.ICGtesting.com
Printed in the USA
BVOW06s1151080316

439509BV00019B/84/P